Francis Frith's
Sherborne

Photographic Memories

Francis Frith's
Sherborne

Nicola Darling-Finan

FRITH
BOOK Co

First published in the United Kingdom in 2001 by
Frith Book Company Ltd

Paperback Edition 2001
ISBN 1-85937-301-1

British Library Cataloguing in Publication Data

Francis Frith's Sherborne
Nicola Darling-Finan

Frith Book Company Ltd
Frith's Barn, Teffont,
Salisbury, Wiltshire SP3 5QP
Tel: +44 (0) 1722 716 376
Email: info@francisfrith.co.uk
www.francisfrith.co.uk

Printed and bound in Great Britain

Front Cover: Sherborne, Cheap Street 1903 49719

AS WITH ANY HISTORICAL DATABASE THE FRITH ARCHIVE IS CONSTANTLY BEING CORRECTED AND IMPROVED
AND THE PUBLISHERS WOULD WELCOME INFORMATION ON OMISSIONS OR INACCURACIES

Contents

Francis Frith: *Victorian Pioneer*

FRANCIS FRITH, Victorian founder of the world-famous photographic archive, was a complex and multi-talented man. A devout Quaker and a highly successful Victorian businessman, he was both philosophic by nature and pioneering in outlook.

By 1855 Francis Frith had already established a wholesale grocery business in Liverpool, and sold it for the astonishing sum of £200,000, which is the equivalent today of over £15,000,000. Now a multi-millionaire, he was able to indulge his passion for travel. As a child he had pored over travel books written by early explorers, and his fancy and imagination had been stirred by family holidays to the sublime mountain regions of Wales and Scotland. 'What a land of spirit-stirring and enriching scenes and places!' he had written. He was to return to these scenes of grandeur in later years to 'recapture the thousands of vivid and tender memories', but with a different purpose. Now in his thirties, and captivated by the new science of photography, Frith set out on a series of pioneering journeys to the Nile regions that occupied him from 1856 until 1860.

Intrigue and Adventure

He took with him on his travels a specially-designed wicker carriage that acted as both dark-room and sleeping chamber. These far-flung journeys were packed with intrigue and adventure. In his life story, written when he was sixty-three, Frith tells of being held captive by bandits, and of fighting 'an awful midnight battle to the very point of surrender with a deadly pack of hungry, wild dogs'. Sporting flowing Arab costume, Frith arrived at Akaba by camel seventy years before Lawrence, where he encountered 'desert princes and rival sheikhs, blazing with jewel-hilted swords'.

During these extraordinary adventures he was assiduously exploring the desert regions bordering the Nile and patiently recording the antiquities and peoples with his camera. He was the first photographer to venture beyond the sixth cataract. Africa was still the mysterious 'Dark Continent', and Stanley and Livingstone's historic meeting was a decade into the future. The conditions for picture taking confound belief. He laboured for hours in his wicker dark-room in the sweltering heat of the desert, while the volatile chemicals fizzed dangerously in their trays. Often he was forced to work in remote tombs and caves where conditions were cooler. Back in London he exhibited his photographs and was 'rapturously cheered' by members of the Royal Society. His reputation as a photographer was made overnight. An eminent modern historian has likened their impact on the population of the time to that on our own generation of the first photographs taken on the surface of the moon.

Venture of a Life-Time

Characteristically, Frith quickly spotted the opportunity to create a new business as a specialist publisher of photographs. He lived in an era of immense and sometimes violent change. For the poor in the early part of Victoria's reign work was a drudge and the hours long, and people had precious little free time to enjoy themselves. Most had no transport other than a cart or gig at their disposal, and had not travelled far beyond the boundaries of their own town or village. However,

by the 1870s, the railways had threaded their way across the country, and Bank Holidays and half-day Saturdays had been made obligatory by Act of Parliament. All of a sudden the ordinary working man and his family were able to enjoy days out and see a little more of the world.

With characteristic business acumen, Francis Frith foresaw that these new tourists would enjoy having souvenirs to commemorate their days out. In 1860 he married Mary Ann Rosling and set out with the intention of photographing every city, town and village in Britain. For the next thirty years he travelled the country by train and by pony and trap, producing fine photographs of seaside resorts and beauty spots that were keenly bought by millions of Victorians. These prints were painstakingly pasted into family albums and pored over during the dark nights of winter, rekindling precious memories of summer excursions.

The Rise of Frith & Co

Frith's studio was soon supplying retail shops all over the country. To meet the demand he gathered about him a small team of photographers, and published the work of independent artist-photographers of the calibre of Roger Fenton and Francis Bedford. In order to gain some understanding of the scale of Frith's business one only has to look at the catalogue issued by Frith & Co in 1886: it runs to some 670 pages, listing not only many thousands of views of the British Isles but also many photographs of most European countries, and China, Japan, the USA and Canada – note the sample page shown above from the hand-written *Frith & Co* ledgers detailing pictures taken. By 1890 Frith had created the greatest specialist photographic publishing company in the world,

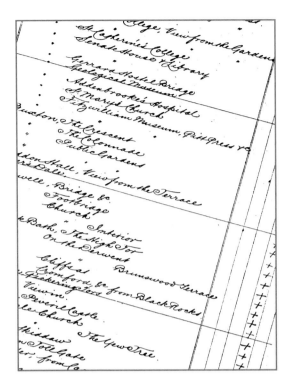

Frith's death, a new card measuring 5.5 x 3.5 inches became the standard format, but it was not until 1902 that the divided back came into being, with address and message on one face and a full-size illustration on the other. *Frith & Co* were in the vanguard of postcard development, and Frith's sons Eustace and Cyril continued their father's monumental task, expanding the number of views offered to the public and recording more and more places in Britain, as the coasts and countryside were opened up to mass travel.

Francis Frith died in 1898 at his villa in Cannes, his great project still growing. The archive he created continued in business for another seventy years. By 1970 it contained over a third of a million pictures of 7,000 cities, towns and villages. The massive photographic record Frith has left to us stands as a living monument to a special and very remarkable man.

with over 2,000 outlets – more than the combined number that Boots and W H Smith have today! The picture on the right shows the *Frith & Co* display board at Ingleton in the Yorkshire Dales. Beautifully constructed with mahogany frame and gilt inserts, it could display up to a dozen local scenes.

Postcard Bonanza

The ever-popular holiday postcard we know today took many years to develop. In 1870 the Post Office issued the first plain cards, with a pre-printed stamp on one face. In 1894 they allowed other publishers' cards to be sent through the mail with an attached adhesive halfpenny stamp. Demand grew rapidly, and in 1895 a new size of postcard was permitted called the court card, but there was little room for illustration. In 1899, a year after

Frith's Archive: *A Unique Legacy*

FRANCIS FRITH'S legacy to us today is of immense significance and value, for the magnificent archive of evocative photographs he created provides a unique record of change in 7,000 cities, towns and villages throughout Britain over a century and more. Frith and his fellow studio photographers revisited locations many times down the years to update their views, compiling for us an enthralling and colourful pageant of British life and character.

We tend to think of Frith's sepia views of Britain as nostalgic, for most of us use them to conjure up memories of places in our own lives with which we have family associations. It often makes us forget that to Francis Frith they were records of daily life as it was actually being lived in the cities, towns and villages of his day. The Victorian age was one of great and often bewildering change for ordinary people, and though the pictures evoke an impression of slower times, life was as busy and hectic as it is today.

We are fortunate that Frith was a photographer of the people, dedicated to recording the minutiae of everyday life. For it is this sheer wealth of visual data, the painstaking chronicle of changes in dress, transport, street layouts, buildings, housing, engineering and landscape that captivates us so much today. His remarkable images offer us a powerful link with the past and with the lives of our ancestors.

Today's Technology

Computers have now made it possible for Frith's many thousands of images to be accessed almost instantly. In the Frith archive today, each photograph is carefully 'digitised' then stored on a CD Rom. Frith archivists can locate a single photograph amongst thousands within seconds. Views can be catalogued and sorted under a variety of categories of place and content to the immediate benefit of researchers.

Inexpensive reference prints can be created for them at the touch of a mouse button, and a wide range of books and other printed materials assembled and published for a wider, more general readership - in the next twelve months over a hundred Frith local history titles will be published! The day-to-day workings of the archive are very different from how they were in Francis Frith's time: imagine the herculean task of sorting through eleven tons of glass negatives as Frith had to do to locate a particular sequence of pictures! Yet

See Frith at www.francisfrith.co.uk

the archive still prides itself on maintaining the same high standards of excellence laid down by Francis Frith, including the painstaking cataloguing and indexing of every view.

It is curious to reflect on how the internet now allows researchers in America and elsewhere greater instant access to the archive than Frith himself ever enjoyed. Many thousands of individual views can be called up on screen within seconds on one of the Frith internet sites, enabling people living continents away to revisit the streets of their ancestral home town, or view places in Britain where they have enjoyed holidays. Many overseas researchers welcome the chance to view special theme selections, such as transport, sports, costume and ancient monuments.

We are certain that Francis Frith would have heartily approved of these modern developments in imaging techniques, for he himself was always working at the very limits of Victorian photographic technology.

The Value of the Archive Today

Because of the benefits brought by the computer, Frith's images are increasingly studied by social historians, by researchers into genealogy and ancestory, by architects, town planners, and by teachers and schoolchildren involved in local history projects.

In addition, the archive offers every one of us an opportunity to examine the places where we and our families have lived and worked down the years. Highly successful in Frith's own era, the archive is now, a century and more on, entering a new phase of popularity.

The Past in Tune with the Future

Historians consider the Francis Frith Collection to be of prime national importance. It is the only archive of its kind remaining in private ownership and has been valued at a million pounds. However, this figure is now rapidly increasing as digital technology enables more and more people around the world to enjoy its benefits.

Francis Frith's archive is now housed in an historic timber barn in the beautiful village of Teffont in Wiltshire. Its founder would not recognize the archive office as it is today. In place of the many thousands of dusty boxes containing glass plate negatives and an all-pervading odour of photographic chemicals, there are now ranks of computer screens. He would be amazed to watch his images travelling round the world at unimaginable speeds through network and internet lines.

The archive's future is both bright and exciting. Francis Frith, with his unshakeable belief in making photographs available to the greatest number of people, would undoubtedly approve of what is being done today with his lifetime's work. His photographs, depicting our shared past, are now bringing pleasure and enlightenment to millions around the world a century and more after his death.

Sherborne - *An Introduction*

THE HISTORIC ABBEY TOWN of Sherborne derives its name from two old English words, Scir meaning 'clear' and Burne, a brook or spring; the town has also been known as Shere Bourn. In the early days the monks referred to it as Fons Clarus or Fons Limpidus. Evidence of a Roman settlement was found at Lenthay, when a villa and pavements were uncovered. The town can be traced as the place where St Aldhelm set the seat of the Bishopric of the newer Wessex, which was originally under the ecclesiastical jurisdiction of the West Saxon Bishop at Winchester - then Bishop Haedde (676-703). Aldhelm, educated at Canterbury, had built churches at Malmesbury, Bruton and Wareham, and monasteries at Frome and Bradford. In 705, following a division of lands by King Ina after the death of Haedde (who had been against such a division), a new diocese was created and Aldhelm, Abbot of Malmesbury, was appointed the first Bishop of the West Saxons. Winchester was the chief town and capital of the entire West Saxon kingdom, but from 705, Sherborne held the second place as part of 'Newer Wessex'. Aldhelm was Bishop for only four years, dying in 709.

In 845 Bishop Eahlstan of Sherborne (a general to King Ethelwulf) defeated the Danes in a battle at the mouth of the River Parret. A few years later, Winchester was deemed unsafe because of the threat posed by the Danes, so, for a brief period between 860 and 878, Sherborne became the capital of the West Saxon kingdom. In 855 Ethelwulf gave up the Kingdom of Wessex to his son Ethelbald and died three years later. He was first buried at Steyning in Sussex, but his body was later removed

to Winchester. On the death of his father Ethelbald became King in his own right and later married his stepmother, Judith, daughter of Charles the Bald, King of the Franks. After much disapproval by the Church of this 'incestuous' relationship, the couple were forcibly separated. Ethelbald died in 860, and was buried in Sherborne Abbey. The dead king's successor, Ethelbert, like his father, had been sub-king in Kent, Essex, Sussex and Surrey. There is no record of any marriage and he died in 865, also being buried in Sherborne Abbey. The next brother to succeed was Ethelred I, who spent the entire six years of his reign in conflict with the Danish invaders; between 871 and 933, three Bishops of Sherborne were defeated in battle against the Danes: Heahmund, Werstan and Sigelm. In a battle at Merton in 871, Ethelred was fatally wounded and was buried in Wimborne Minster. Despite having two sons (Ethelhelm - who was later to become Archbishop of Canterbury - and Ethelwold) he was succeeded by King Alfred the Great.

An entry in the Domesday Book reads: "The Bishop himself hold Sherborne. Eddid the Queen held it and before her, Bishop Alward. In King Edward's time it gelded for 43 hides. There was land for 46 plough teams."

Sherborne Cathedral served St Aldhelm and a further 26 Saxon Bishops, although after the Norman Conquest the Bishop's seat was transferred to Old Sarum and then to Salisbury. In 998 St Wulfsin requested that the monks of the Order of St Benedict come to the Abbey where they remained until it was surrendered in 1539 to King Henry VIII during the Dissolution.

During the Norman period, the Abbey was considerably altered and rebuilt and later, in the 13th century, the east end saw the addition of a Lady Chapel. In the 15th century the Abbey again underwent much restoration, which was commenced under John Brunyng, who was abbot from 1415 to 1436. During major mid-Victorian renovations it was decided, following a Board of Health Report, that the parish graveyard had to be closed as a health hazard; the Lenthay cemetery was opened in 1856.

For centuries the town has been famous for its schools and especially, of course, Sherborne School, known locally as King's. There is evidence that schooling here was in existence as early as the 12th century, and possibly as far back as the early 8th century, and the school even continued through the trials of the Reformation. In 1550 came the Grant of its Charter and endowment by Edward VI, from whence came its title, King Edward VI Free Grammar School, by which it was known until 1922. The School was largely centred around the Abbey grounds, but later various buildings were acquired around the town.

Standing proudly side-by-side are the two castles of Sherborne; the old and the new. The Old Castle was commenced by Bishop Roger de Caen in 1108, but in 1139 he was forced by King Stephen to

surrender it to the Crown. By 1217 the castle had passed to the Earl of Salisbury, a move which was to prove a source of dispute over many years. In 1355 Robert Wyville, Bishop of Sarum, claiming that the transfer had been fraudulent, requested a duel to settle the matter. This proved unnecessary when the King (Edward III) ordered the Earl of Salisbury to give up the castle to the Bishop.

At the end of the 16th century, the castle was in the possession of Queen Elizabeth I, it having been given to the Crown by John Coldwell, Bishop of Sarum. Elizabeth granted the castle to Sir Walter Raleigh who, after much labour, gave up the effort of trying to modernise it and built instead what we know today as the New Sherborne Castle. On 21 September 1603, Raleigh was indicted for High Treason and conspiring against James I. He was found guilty but was released by the King in 1616 to go to the Orinoco in search of gold. He returned to his arrest two years later and was executed in Old Palace Yard, Westminster on 29 October 1618, on the original charges of 1603.

The Old Castle famously became a ruin as a result of Civil War action during 1642 and 1645. In 1645 the castle fell after a 16-day siege when Sir Lewis Dives attempted to hold out against General Fairfax and Cromwell. Sadly this episode took its toll on the old building.

An annual event, popular among locals and visitors alike, is Pack Monday Fair. Held on the first Monday after Old Michaelmas Day, the Fair takes place around the second week in October. From 1560 to 1748, in return for an annual payment, the Governors of Sherborne School rented the Fairs and Market Place from the Lord of Sherborne Manor. Pack Monday, or St Michell's, Fair was one of three medieval fairs, the others being known as 'the Fair on the Grene' and Castletoun Fair. Pack Monday is greeted by a procession at midnight of Teddy Roe's Band - the origins of this are uncertain but the idea is thought to originate from a pagan ritual. The Fair was partly a livestock market and, with the addition of stalls selling all manner of merchandise - foods, sweets, linens, lace, pottery and the like, must have been a fine day out, eagerly anticipated by buyers and sellers from far and wide. Today, the Fair is still popular although livestock trading ceased several years ago.

Sherborne has been a busy industrial town in many ways, not least in the silk business. In the mid-18th century, a silk thrower by the name of John Sharrer moved to the town from Whitechapel. Finding no shortage of labour in the town, he set up his business there, acquiring premises and land at Westbury. Raw silk was brought to Sherborne from many places including China, Turkey, Spain and Italy. The silk was processed in throwing mills where it was cleaned ready for use. Sharrer died in 1767, having been responsible for bringing the business of silk throwing to Sherborne. The industry continued, although not without trials and tribulations and by the end of the 19th century it

was in decline. The silk mill closed in 1885. Happily, it was soon to reopen and an improvement in pay and conditions was forthcoming. Queen Victoria was a customer at the end of the century, ordering lengths of silk in 1897, her Diamond Jubilee. By the beginning of the 20th century, the business was thriving again and the future was looking bright. Following further difficulties before the Second World War, the mill was purchased by Frederick Marsden who was to change the face of the company. Astutely, he tendered for the supply of silk parachutes and material for the electrical industry during the War, and by 1942, following this success, Marsden diversified. After extensive research, production began of the mill's first glass fibre fabric, known in the electrical industry, which purchased the material, as 'Marsden's Glass' and later 'Marglass'. Could the 18th-century businessman John Sharrer ever have anticipated that the beginnings of his work in Sherborne all those years ago would culminate in such well-known products in the future?

Sherborne was no stranger to tragedy during the Second World War and its proximity to Yeovilton and Westlands made its situation a dangerous one. On Monday 30 September 1940,

50 German bombers came under attack from Yeovil and promptly switched their target to Sherborne. In less than five minutes, 300 bombs had been dropped on the town, killing 18 people and injuring 32. Among the sites bombed were: Lenthay, Cheap Street, Half Moon Street, Abbey Road and Sherborne School (with three bombs landing in the Courts), Newland, North Road, The Avenue, Tinney's Lane, Acreman Street, Richmond Road and the Horsecastles area. Then, on 24 March 1944, an explosion in Sherborne Park killed 43 American soldiers; an army lorry had been accidentally driven over a landmine and, being in an area holding much ammunition, set off several other explosives. A memorial to these men can be seen near the War Memorial in Half Moon Street.

In the 21st century, Sherborne remains unspoilt, having lost none of its charm, and the beautiful buildings that make up the town stand as a testament to the quality of local work from centuries gone by. Despite the frantic activity which the 21st century life seems to entail, Sherborne keeps that aura of tranquility which today is lost in so many English towns.

From the Slopes 1887
19660

On 7 May 1860, Sherborne Railway Station was opened. There were great celebrations with the first London train departing at 6.30am. How the Victorian residents must have marvelled, if somewhat nervously, that London could be reached from Sherborne in as little as two hours! Due to lack of funding and disputes over the proposed route, the railway came to Sherborne later than at first anticipated; the first meeting to discuss the proposition had been held in 1846, although work did not start until 1858. As with most towns, the advent of the railway in Sherborne made the town more accessible and changed the lives of many people.

Sherborne, From the Slopes 1891 29638
In this late Victorian view across the town, a gasholder features prominently on the left. The Gas Works was installed in 1836 and soon the inhabitants of Sherborne were enjoying the many benefits of 'modern' fuel. Initially, the streets were only lit between October and April. In the distance can be seen the Abbey and, on the left, the Digby Hotel. Nearby is the site which was soon to become Pageant Gardens.

Sherborne, Digby Road 1891 29639
The view shows Digby Road and the Digby Hotel. This hotel was built by George Digby Wingfield Digby and it opened on Pack Monday, 11 October 1869. An Assembly Room was added in 1878. The Hotel was popular and a cab was even provided to transport guests from the railway, a distance of no more than a few hundred yards! The hotel was sold to the Saunders family in 1900 and they later opened a motor garage from the original stable block in Digby Road. When the hotel finally closed, it was bought by Sherborne School and recommenced life as a boarding house in 1962. The river in the foreground is the River Yeo.

Sherborne, From the Slopes 1891 29637
A view of Sherborne with Gas House Hill running down to meet the railway line from New Road.

Sherborne, From the Slopes 1895 37076
The level crossing gates are shut in anticipation of a train. The Woolmington Hotel is seen, built in the 1860s for Mr Woolmington, owner of the Cheap Street Brewery. This was later to become the Pageant.

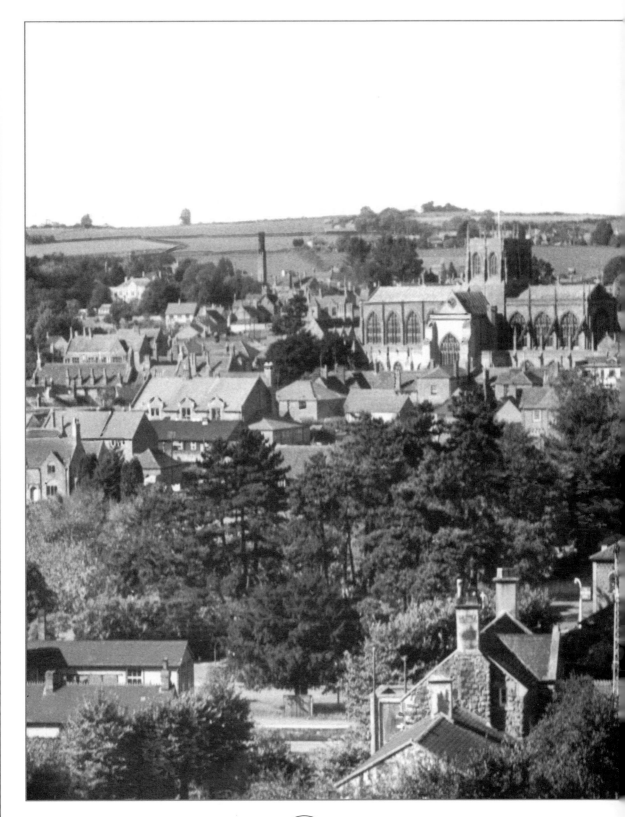

**Sherborne
From the Slopes
c1955** S112097
Taken from the same
spot as photograph
number 37076,
although 60 years later.
While buildings and
businesses come and
go over the years, the
general landscape and
topography changes
little and this view today,
at the beginning of the
21st century, remains
much the same.

◄ **Newell c1955** S112029
Looking from Newell up to Greenhill with the Crown Hotel on the left. The Crown has changed little since this photograph was taken although the parking facilities have increased on the road at the front of the building. The turning on the right, in front of the pedestrian, leads to Back Lane and the Yeatman Hospital.

◄ Yeovil Road 1900 46084
Looking towards Newell at the turn of the century. The road on the right is Cornhill leading onto Acreman Street. The houses on the left are no longer there, having been demolished in the 1950s. The road on that side is the Marston Road. In medieval times this area was known as Barton Cross.

▼ Newell c1955 S112133
Looking in the opposite direction from S112029, towards Yeovil and Kitt Hill. The buildings on the left are Kitt Hill House and Newell House, the former being opened as a boarding school as early as 1757.

◄ Greenhill 1900 46083
Until mid-Victorian times, this part of the road, known now as Greenhill, had been called New Well Hill. Here, we are looking towards the Green at the turn of the century. This scene has changed little over 100 years although it is never this quiet today with much traffic on the main A30.

▼ Greenhill c1955 S112134

Looking west down the hill with some 'modern' streetlighting. Until the 1950s, the wall surrounding Newell House, at the bottom of Greenhill opposite the Crown Hotel, was an accident blackspot and had to be demolished, providing the grassy verge we know today.

▼ The Green c1955 S112135

This was the site of much activity, including horse fairs, which continued regularly until the mid-20th century. The Green is today architecturally unchanged from this photograph. The large building in the centre was formerly known as the Angel Inn and, as the sign above the door still testifies today, was 'Licensed To Let Post Horses'. This was on the main route to London, Bath, Bristol, Exeter and Cornwall and was, naturally, very busy. The building eventually became a boarding house for Sherborne School. The traffic island marks the site of a wartime water tank.

▲ The Avenue 1904 51330

In the 19th century, this road was known as Coldharbour Lane and was built up as the Avenue during the Victorian and Edwardian periods. Hill House, on the left, was built for the Reverend Arthur Field in 1899. In 1978 the grounds were used for building and the development known as Hill House Close was born. At the 'top' end of the Avenue stands Quarry House, built in 1924 for the writer Littleton Powys, designed by his architect brother Albert Powys. The road in the distance bends to the left and emerges into Newland.

◀ Newland Manor 1904
51340

Many inhabitants have come and gone over the 500 or so years this building has stood here. 'Manor' is a misnomer as the house was never such. In late Victorian times the building housed a ladies' school and today is the offices of the West Dorset District Council and Sherborne Town Council. The wall to the right no longer stands and there is now access through here to a car park at the rear of the building.

Sherborne House 1904 51342
This splendid house was built for Henry Seymour Portman in about 1720. The architect was Benjamin Bastard. The staircase murals were painted by Sir James Thornhill, Hogarth's father-in-law. Other famous connections include William Charles Macready, the Victorian actor, who lived here between 1850 and 1860, and some of his house guests, among them Charles Dickens and William Thackeray.

The Yeatman Hospital 1895 37089
The Yeatman Hospital in Hospital Lane was completed in 1864 at a total cost of £2000; the foundation stone was laid by Mrs Wingfield Digby. Named after the Reverend Harry Farr Yeatman, the hospital opened on 19 March 1866 and today is still serving the local people. Further additions and enlargements to the hospital occurred in 1913, 1927, 1939 and 1965.

Higher Cheap Street c1955 S112101
The building behind the pillar box, seen here as Peter, Sherston & Wylam, land agents, is now an antique shop and
the business to the left now a Bistro. The George Hotel, dating back to the early 16th century, still stands here.
The building itself was in existence as early as the beginning of the 15th century. In the distance, at the top of
Higher Cheap Street, can be seen the Antelope Hotel in Greenhill. This area is rarely so free of traffic these days!

Cheap Street c1965 S112136
In this 1960s view of the top of Cheap Street can be seen the White Hart public house; the area known today as
Blackmore Vale was previously called the Vale of the White Hart. The sign outside the pub is advertising Toby Ale.
A bus typical of the period is waiting at what is still today a bus stop.

Thomas a Beckett's Chapel 1904 51345
'La Julianys Inne', named after St Julian of Norwich, was given to the Almshouse by Margaret Goffe in 1437. This is the later 16th-century building. The built-up triangular stone in the corner, which can be better seen in photograph 64652, was a device installed to try to prevent gentlemen answering the call of nature here. The archway on the left led to the old George Yard and is now part of George Street.

Cheap Street 1912 64652
Looking on a wet day from Higher Cheap Street outside the George. The turning on the left leads into Newland.
Almost 100 years later this scene has hardly changed.

Cheap Street c1955 S112090
The business on the left is now Balfour newsagents and next to this is a fish and chip and wet fish shop. Beyond,
the Greyhound is no longer there. On the site of the old Woolmington Brewery now stands a new development of
apartments known as Woolmington's Yard.

Cheap Street c1955 S112004
The Sherborne Gas Showrooms is no longer there. It was to become Automotives, for car parts and accessories, and later still, Stanley Racing. Earlier in its life it had been Chaffin's the photographer, who had a business here until the 1930s when it was transferred to South Street. The motor car in the distance would no longer be able to drive up the street since it is now part of a one-way system.

Cheap Street 1927 80337
Coombs' Restaurant, seen here in its original form, was redesigned in 1935. The bakery remained here until the early 1960s and is now the site of Woolworth's. Earlier still had stood C A Ford, Hygienic Steam Bakery & Restaurant. The Tudor building on the left, seen here as Bown & Sons, was largely altered in the 1960s and is now occupied by the National Westminster Bank.

▼ **Cheap Street c1955** S112091

Some well-known names here, although not in the same places as today: Boots and Woolworth's have moved further up Cheap Street. Barclays Bank on the corner of Hound Street is still in the same place. Also seen here are Bollom dry cleaners and the International Stores. On the left is the Abbey Bookshop Ltd and the Abbey Press. The business of printing survived here from the mid-19th century until 1987. The Abbey Bookshop and newsagents still occupies the site.

▼ **Sherborne**
Cheap Street 1891 29652

We are now looking up Cheap Street with the Conduit on the left. On the corner of Cheap Street and Long Street is Penny's ironmongers and furnishers, later to become Durrant's grocers.

▲ **Cheap Street 1903**
49719

On the corner of Cheap Street and Long Street is the previously-mentioned Durrant's grocers. The proprietor was several times Chairman of the Urban District Council and Durrant's Close is named after him. Their advertisement of the time read: 'Vans to all parts of the district daily. Special terms for Hotels, Schools and Large Consumers'. Between 1837 and 1938, Durrant's Close at Horsecastles was the site of the Sherborne Union Workhouse. A horse and cart delivering milk is seen here with several milk churns aboard. Often the vendor also offered eggs and cheese, carried in wooden boxes.

◀ Cheap Street c1955

S112096

On the left is the Westminster Bank and on the corner of Cheap Street and Long Street is Milward's Shoes; a shoe shop is still on these premises today. The market is busy operating in the Parade and the 'No Entry' signs show that Cheap Street has become part of the one-way system.

South Street 1887

19670

The shop facing us on the left, stood at the corner of Half Moon Street and Cheap Street, and was the business of Robert Adams, watch and clockmaker. Four years after the photograph was taken, this building was demolished to facilitate road widening at this point. The building which replaced it, St John's House, built for the Almshouse of St John the Baptist and St John the Evangelist, was for some time occupied by the Urban District Council. On the right, in the foreground, is the Sherborne Iron, Steel and Hardware Company (late W Parsons). Robert Adams subsequently moved to premises in Cheap Street where he advertised as 'Watchmaker, Jeweller, Silversmith and Optician'.

Half Moon Street c1955 S112033
On the right hand side, several businesses, including Pedley & White outfitters, occupy the Church House building, erected in the 1530s on the site of old tenements. The ground floor space was occupied by shops while the upper was used for meetings. At the end of the 17th century, the Church House, under the charge of the Almshouse, was divided and became three separate tenements. The three obviously different roofs seen in the photograph show exactly how the separation was made.

◄ Half Moon Street 1904 51329

Phillips & Handover is seen here on the left, looking along Half Moon Street towards the Almshouse. Several hats and garments are displayed outside the shop. The horse and cart is waiting, untethered, for its owner. The building on the right is the new one which replaced Adams' clockmaker.

▼ Half Moon Hotel c1955 S112121

In the distance on the left is the Plume of Feathers and, comparing with photograph 51329, a change can be seen. In April 1936, the owners of the Half Moon Hotel purchased the neighbouring premises of Dingley's, drapers, outfitters, milliners and hosiers, and soon the new building had been redesigned and built as we see it today, set back from the road and occupying a large part of this side of the street. Also demolished at this time was Cross's ironmongers.

◄ Half Moon Street c1955 S112095

Looking east, we see on the left the businesses of W Warr & Son, hairdressing and chiropody, and Pedley & White, drapers and outfitters. In the distance is Greenham's butchers. Next to this is Frisby's, a well-known shoe chain.

Half Moon Street 1903 49720
Looking east again along Half Moon Street with the Abbey on the left and the entrance to Digby Road on the right. In the distance can be seen Tuffin's Tea Rooms situated behind the Church House. It was approximately in the centre of this view that the Town Hall had once stood. In common with many other town halls, the Sherborne building was built to include a market and corn exchange and to house the Assizes. Built in 1681, and in regular use for assemblies and meetings, dinners and entertainment, the Town Hall was demolished in 1884.

Long Street 1924 75950
Records of the existence of this street go back at least to the 15th century and it is known to have been used by travellers and pilgrims on their way to the Abbey. On the left-hand side of this street stood the buildings belonging to the Long Street Brewery which can be identified here as the tall building in the distance. The Dorsetshire Brewery (Sherborne) Ltd, later to be known as Thorne's, had been established in 1796 and ended its days under the name of Baxter's. This site was redeveloped in the 1980s as The Maltings, a residential complex.

Long Street 1891 29654

A splendid 1890s scene showing several different styles of fine architecture synonymous with this historic town. The Conduit, seen here, is a hexagonal structure built in the early 16th century by Abbot John Meere; originally part of the Abbey cloister, it was the monks' washing place. The name 'Conduit' actually refers to the channel or 'way' along which water ran to serve the building itself. The conduit was moved to the Parade in the mid-16th century and has since had several uses including a reading room, a penny bank and a pen operated by the local constabulary. In 1889 the building was set back a short way to its present position. At one time it had been glazed and enclosed by six-foot high iron railings to protect the reading room (and presumably its occupants).

Long Street 1924
75951
This little girl in 1920s Long Street seems to have been sent out with her little sister (or brother) in tow in this very smart perambulator. According to the Abbey clock, it is about five minutes to two in the afternoon.

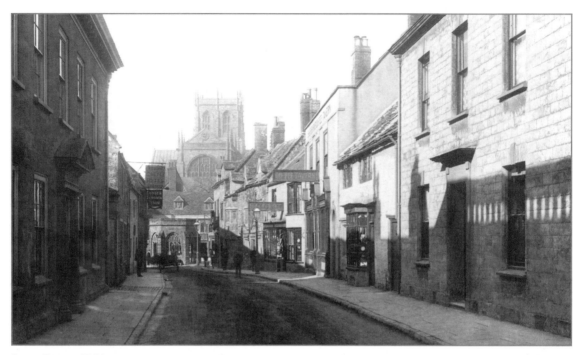

Long Street 1891 29653
This late Victorian photograph shows part of Long Street looking west to the Abbey. Businesses seen here at the time include the Sherborne Coffee Tavern on the right and the Castle Hotel and Rose and Crown on the left.

The Conduit 1924 75947
The Abbey towers in the background in this photograph showing the Parade. The Cross Keys Hotel for 'Bruttons Noted Pale Ales and Beer and Stout' is on the right. The building behind the Conduit had been the Sun Inn until 1916, when it was purchased by Sherborne School and became known as Bow House. That section of the building situated behind the dog on the pavement was also incorporated, having previously been Humphries Cycle Works. The sign attached to the lamp reads 'Motorists are requested not to leave their vehicles in Cheap Street'

The Conduit c1955 S112092
Taken from almost the same spot in Long Street as photograph 75947; a signpost has appeared, indicating the way to Dorchester, Blandford, Wincanton and Shaftesbury. To the left of the Conduit is Church Lane. At the base of the Conduit is a trough for horses and dogs which had been placed here in 1882.

The Conduit c1955 S112018
A horse and cart wait patiently at the Parade with Milward's Boots and Shoes at the junction of Cheap Street and Long Street.

**Castleton Church
1891** 29657
This area of Sherborne, known as Castleton, became one of two Boroughs in the town (the other being Newland) and had its own church and market. In this photograph a great change to the area has recently occurred: the railway line had been cut through this spot in 1860. Here we see the bridge which had been built out of necessity at this point. Several houses had been demolished in the process, although happily, arrangements were made to rehouse the occupants.

Castleton Church 1891 29656
A view in the opposite direction showing the castle ruins in the background and a couple of Victorian children keeping an eye on the photographer. The Church is on the left.

Castleton Church 1924 75972
The Church of St Mary Magdalen was built in 1715. The original church bearing this name had been built by Bishop Roger de Caen in the 12th century but was later demolished by Sir Walter Raleigh. A new church replaced it in 1601, but little more than 100 years passed before it too was replaced by the present building, designed and built by the 5th Lord Digby.

Castleton Church 1924 75971
Castleton Church is on the left and, on the right, the three houses
known as Lattice House, Middle House and Raleigh Lodge.

The Castle Entrance Gate 1886 13845

The Old Castle Ruins 1900 46082
This pair of photographs shows the three-storey castle gatehouse of Norman construction with the addition of Tudor windows. In the earlier photograph, a young lady is enjoying her walk up to the castle as countless people have done over the years.

The Old Castle 1904

51347

To give an idea of the immense size of the castle, the keep comprised a basement plus two further storeys, totalling a height of 70 feet with walls nine feet thick. It was on this spot that the Sherborne Pageant of 1905 was held.

The Castle Courtyard 1886 13847

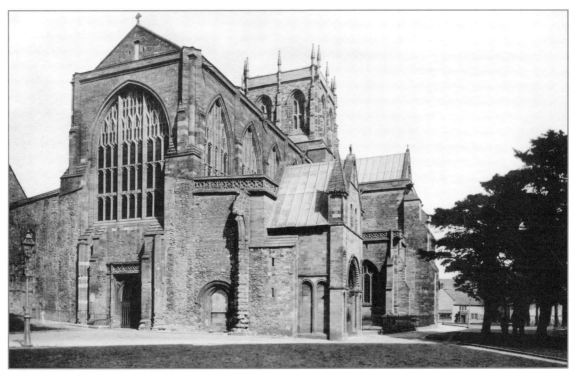

The Abbey 1887 19662

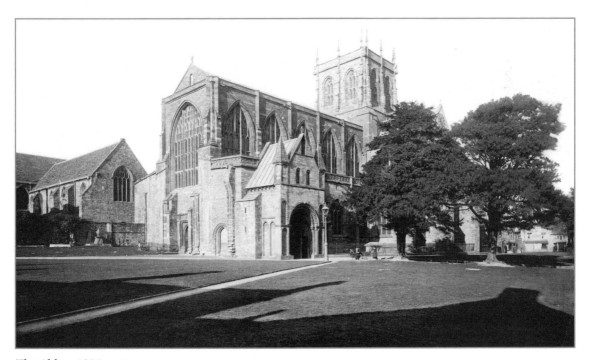

The Abbey 1891 29642
Two views of the Abbey from the west (1887) and the south-west. In the latter, to the left stand Guesten Hall and the King's School Chapel.

The Abbey Chapel c1955 S112073
These two photographs show the south view of the medieval Lady Chapel which, for 300 years (from 1560 to 1860) had been converted for use as the Headmaster's House. The gateposts on the right mark the way into Church Lane. The building on the far right was known as the Laundry Buildings; at one time providing school boarding accommodation, it later became Otton's Temperance Commercial Hotel and was demolished in 1920.

The Abbey, East End 1887 19664

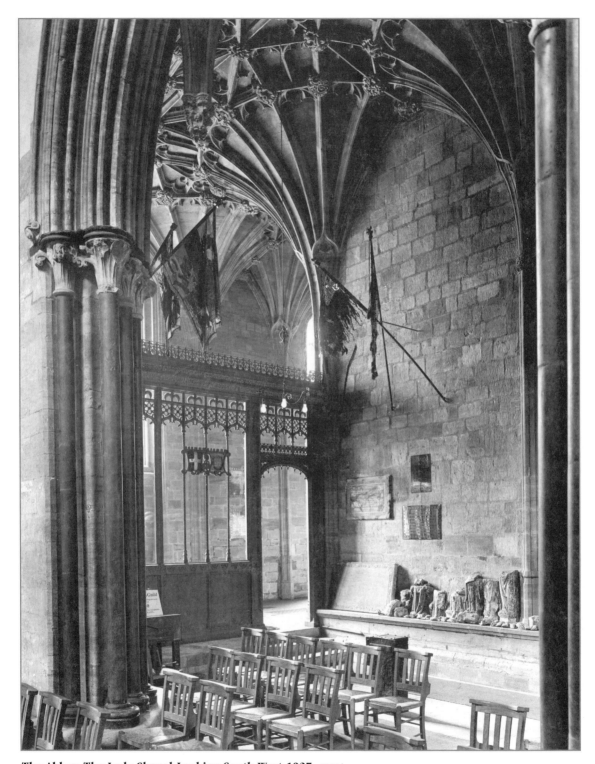

The Abbey, The Lady Chapel Looking South West 1927 80334
How strange to imagine this being part of one's living quarters. This chapel formed part of the Headmaster's accommodation until 1860 (see 19664 and S112073). Above is the splendid 15th-century fan vault.

The Abbey, Nave East 1887 19665
Another glimpse at the Abbey interior. This splendid and imposing architecture shows just how gifted the people were who worked on the construction of the Abbey in the days well before the modern equipment and techniques we know today.

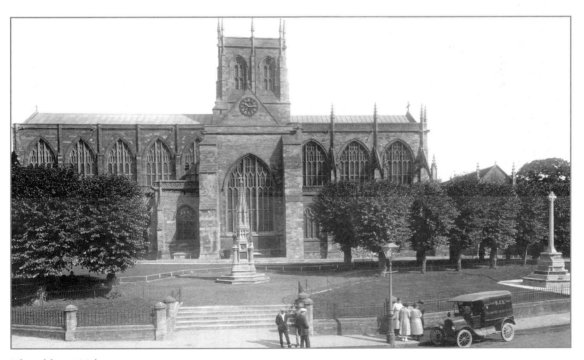

The Abbey 1924 75941
Looking towards the Abbey with the Digby Memorial in front and the newly-erected War Memorial on the right. The delivery van parked here is advertising 'The United Yeast Co Ltd - Pure DCL Yeast'.

The Memorial and Almshouse c1955 S112074

The Sherborne War Memorial was unveiled on 11 November 1921; it had cost £657 5s 6d. There are also plaques commemorating those locals who were killed in the German air raid on Sherborne in 1940 and the American soldiers who lost their lives in the town. The other memorial seen here is the Digby Memorial, unveiled on 1 July 1885 in memory of George Digby Wingfield Digby. The inscription reads: 'To the memory of George Digby Wingfield Digby of Sherborne Castle who upon succeeding to a noble inheritance made it his first care to complete the restoration of the Abbey Church and after a life of generous beneficence died full of years beloved by all classes of the Community. This monument is erected by Public Subscription. MDCCCLXXXIV.' The monument bears four statuettes in bronze, depicting St Aldhelm, Bishop Roger, Abbot Bradford and Sir Walter Raleigh. In the distance, on the corner of Digby Road is Carter & Co Stores for 'Gilbey's Wines & Spirits', and 'Finest Indian, Ceylon and China Teas'. The shop had previously been Vincent's Supply Stores. It later became a supermarket and is now an opticians. Also seen here is the Almshouse.

The Almshouse 1895 37090
The Sherborne Almshouse was founded in 1437. Like many almshouses, this charity was funded largely through rents from the many properties owned by the organisation. The Almshouse of St John the Baptist and St John the Evangelist provided for 'Twelve pore, feeble and ympotent old men and four old women'. The main part of the building was constructed in 1448 and enlarged in the 1860s. At the time of this photograph the female occupants would have worn scarlet cloaks and poke bonnets, and the men, caped coats and shovel hats.

The King's School, Quadrangle 1891 29646
A view of Sherborne School Courts showing the former Abbot's house and kitchen. The monastic kitchen dates from the end of the 15th century and its chimney is seen here. The semi-octagonal building housed the staircase to the Abbot's house. Until the mid-19th century, the building was a private house but it became school property in 1851 and was converted into boys' studies for School House. It was here that four bombs fell during the Second World War.

◄ **The Headmaster's House 1900** 46086
This fine building adjoining School House was built at the same time, 1860. Until this date, the Master's House had been part of the Abbey Lady Chapel (see photographs S112073 and 19664). The castellated extension was added in the early 1880s.

The Old School 1895 37094
The Gothic iron bell cupola stands atop the Bell Building built in 1835 by Ralph Lyon, the school's headmaster from 1823 to 1845.

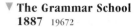

The Grammar School 1887 19672
This photograph, entitled with the school's historic name, King Edward VI Free Grammar School, shows School House, which was built by Hugo Daniel Harper, the school's headmaster from 1850, who required new accommodation for himself and boarding boys. The foundation stone was laid on 26 June 1860 by the Earl of Shaftesbury.

Big School 1903 49718
The building, designed in the Perpendicular style by R H Carpenter, was commenced in 1879. Following bomb damage in the 1940 air raid, the building was altered in 1956; its outward appearance took on an Elizabethan style in contrast to this austere Gothic design. One of the productions of 'Goodbye Mr Chips' was filmed here in 1968.

**The King's School
The Library 1900**
46075
An interesting peep
inside the school library
showing row upon row
of orderly volumes, with
the side windows
providing much light for
reading and studying.

▼ The School Cloisters 1924 75967

Over the years, the Gothic style and shadowy appearance afforded by this fine architecture have led to several claims that these cloisters are haunted. Probably many a boy cutting along here after nightfall has felt somewhat unnerved.

▼ The School and Gateway 1924 75959

The entrance to the Courts through the Gate Tower, designed by Sir Reginald Blomfield in 1923. The arms above the entrance depict a Tudor-style Welsh dragon. The gate on the left is the entrance to the small churchyard behind the Methodist Church.

▲ The Abbey House 1904
51336

This building in Abbey Road had been the Abbey School for the Poor, or National School. It had undergone major rebuilding and extending by the time this photograph was taken in 1904, having joined forces in 1887 with Abbey House (just seen to the right of this main building), to serve as a boarding house for the King's School. The Abbey House suffered a disastrous fire on the night of 7-8 July 1962. It was brought under control but the building was extensively damaged. It was eventually restored and still stands today.

◄ **Carrington Building 1912** 64654
The Carrington Building opened in 1910 as science laboratories and an art school. Designed by Blomfield, the benefactor was J B Carrington, one of the governors. The foundation stone was laid by Lord Shaftesbury on 8 December 1909. On the right is Big School before its 1956 alterations.

King's School 1912
64655
Looking in the opposite direction to that in photograph 64654. Some boys have stopped with their bicycles to pose for the photographer. The newly-built Carrington Building is now on the right.

The School c1955 S112076
A wider view of the gatehouse in the 1950s. On the left is the newly-built Medlycott history building designed by
Oswald Brakspear.

Harper House 1904 51337
The name Harper House dates from 1910. Situated between Hound Street and Long Street, and previously known
as The Retreat, boys were admitted from 1873. The building was later to be extended.

The School, Westcott House 1924 75969
Formerly known as Grosvenor Lodge, this building was constructed in about 1800 for the Melmoth family. As Westcott House, it was opened as a boarding house in 1920. The building was enlarged by G O'Hanlon shortly before this photograph was taken. Further enlargements were carried out in the mid 1960s.

Abbeylands, Cheap Street 1900 46085
Rather over-vigorous shrubbery seems to have almost obliterated all trace of the windows and doors here on the Abbeylands Building - the details can be seen more clearly in photograph 51335 on pages 72-3.

Wilson's School 1904
51338
Originally the Angel Inn, (see S112135) this house was acquired by the governors of Sherborne School in 1865. Together with other buildings to the rear, this became a school boarding house, the Green. Thanks to Lord Iliffe, the school owned the property outright from 1929. Today this building has been redeveloped as luxury apartments. Here, some Edwardian young ladies and a horse and trap can be seen at the front of the house.

**Abbeylands
King's School 1904**
51335
The left side of this building (Abbey Road) was occupied by John Cutter, headmaster of Sherborne School from 1790 to 1823. By 1872, it had opened as a boarding house and was eventually purchased by the school governors after World War One. The entrance seen here in the centre can be dated to 1649, although the part of the building giving onto Cheap Street, and at one time a corn merchant's business, is said to date to the 1570s.

▼ **The Head Mistress's House 1904** 51334
Sherborne School for Girls dating from 1899 and founded by Mrs Kenelm Wingfield Digby, is here seen on Bradford Road - its home from 1903. Prior to this, the school had been in Ramsam House at Greenhill.

▼ **The Ladies' College 1912** 64660
To the right of the picture, the present-day clock tower, designed by Sir Reginald Blomfield in 1926, is yet to be added. Here some spectators watch while the girls participate in what looks like a game of cricket or rounders.

▲ **The Ladies' College 1904** 51332
Another view of the school buildings, seen from the opposite side. At this time, this site had only been occupied by the school for no more than a year.

◀ **The School Playing Fields and Old Gateway 1924** 75970
This gateway had previously stood at the bottom of Hospital Lane. When the Tower Gateway of the King's School was erected in 1923, the gateway was removed to the Horsecastles site, where it still stands today.

Pageant Gardens 1906 56386

Pageant Gardens 1912 64651

The Digby Hotel 1924 75954
Two views of the newly-constructed gardens, the second showing a
much more mature park. The imposing building in the background
is the Digby Hotel. The famous Pageant of 1905 was to celebrate
the 1200th anniversary of the founding of the town and bishopric
in 705. This enormous display of history, drama and music was
organised by Louis-Napoleon Parker (1852-1844). The work
involved in arranging and directing over 900 performers and
25,000 spectators, must have been considerable. The spectacle
lasted four days and its own 'centenary' is now imminent.

Pageant Gardens 1912 64650

The Digby Hotel 1924 75954

Pageant Gardens 1912 64651
Originally Half Moon Field and at one time used as the Pack
Monday fairground, this land was given to the town by F J B
Wingfield Digby, in memory of his father. The gardens were paid
for by the profit of the 1905 Sherborne Pageant. The trustees of
the pageant subscribed £800 to the laying out of the grounds, and
the bandstand was the gift of Mr Edward Dingley.

Pageant Gardens 1924 75953V
The attire of this family and the perambulator leave us in no doubt as to the date of the photograph. In the background is a Turkish field gun which had been captured in Palestine on 15 November 1917 by 'B' Squadron of the Dorset Yeomanry. Like many towns in Britain, artefacts such as this were in abundance and this one remained here for some time until removed to the grounds of Sherborne Castle.

The Park
The Waterfall 1904
51352

These few pages contain four views showing the delights of the parkland and woodland around the town. Sir Walter Raleigh's Seat, set close to the medieval Dinney Bridge, afforded Raleigh an important vantage point to the Dorchester Road as well as over the splendid gardens. It is said that it was here a servant, thinking Sir Walter to be 'on fire' whilst smoking his new tobacco, doused him with water. There is also a legend that the ghost of Sir Walter appears at Sherborne Castle on St Michael's Eve, 20 September.

The Park, The Sir Walter Raleigh Seat 1904 51353

Terrace Walk 1895 37091

Yew Tree Walk 1904 51351

Index

Frith Book Co Titles

www.francisfrith.co.uk

The Frith Book Company publishes over 100 new titles each year. A selection of those currently available are listed below. For latest catalogue please contact Frith Book Co.

Town Books 96 pages, approx 100 photos. County and Themed Books 128 pages, approx 150 photos (unless specified). All titles hardback laminated case and jacket except those indicated pb (paperback)

Amersham, Chesham & Rickmansworth (pb)			Derby (pb)	1-85937-367-4	£9.99
	1-85937-340-2	£9.99	Derbyshire (pb)	1-85937-196-5	£9.99
Ancient Monuments & Stone Circles	1-85937-143-4	£17.99	Devon (pb)	1-85937-297-x	£9.99
Aylesbury (pb)	1-85937-227-9	£9.99	Dorset (pb)	1-85937-269-4	£9.99
Bakewell	1-85937-113-2	£12.99	Dorset Churches	1-85937-172-8	£17.99
Barnstaple (pb)	1-85937-300-3	£9.99	Dorset Coast (pb)	1-85937-299-6	£9.99
Bath (pb)	1-85937-419-0	£9.99	Dorset Living Memories	1-85937-210-4	£14.99
Bedford (pb)	1-85937-205-8	£9.99	Down the Severn	1-85937-118-3	£14.99
Berkshire (pb)	1-85937-191-4	£9.99	Down the Thames (pb)	1-85937-278-3	£9.99
Berkshire Churches	1-85937-170-1	£17.99	Down the Trent	1-85937-311-9	£14.99
Blackpool (pb)	1-85937-382-8	£9.99	Dublin (pb)	1-85937-231-7	£9.99
Bognor Regis (pb)	1-85937-431-x	£9.99	East Anglia (pb)	1-85937-265-1	£9.99
Bournemouth	1-85937-067-5	£12.99	East London	1-85937-080-2	£14.99
Bradford (pb)	1-85937-204-x	£9.99	East Sussex	1-85937-130-2	£14.99
Brighton & Hove(pb)	1-85937-192-2	£8.99	Eastbourne	1-85937-061-6	£12.99
Bristol (pb)	1-85937-264-3	£9.99	Edinburgh (pb)	1-85937-193-0	£8.99
British Life A Century Ago (pb)	1-85937-213-9	£9.99	England in the 1880s	1-85937-331-3	£17.99
Buckinghamshire (pb)	1-85937-200-7	£9.99	English Castles (pb)	1-85937-434-4	£9.99
Camberley (pb)	1-85937-222-8	£9.99	English Country Houses	1-85937-161-2	£17.99
Cambridge (pb)	1-85937-422-0	£9.99	Essex (pb)	1-85937-270-8	£9.99
Cambridgeshire (pb)	1-85937-420-4	£9.99	Exeter	1-85937-126-4	£12.99
Canals & Waterways (pb)	1-85937-291-0	£9.99	Exmoor	1-85937-132-9	£14.99
Canterbury Cathedral (pb)	1-85937-179-5	£9.99	Falmouth	1-85937-066-7	£12.99
Cardiff (pb)	1-85937-093-4	£9.99	Folkestone (pb)	1-85937-124-8	£9.99
Carmarthenshire	1-85937-216-3	£14.99	Glasgow (pb)	1-85937-190-6	£9.99
Chelmsford (pb)	1-85937-310-0	£9.99	Gloucestershire	1-85937-102-7	£14.99
Cheltenham (pb)	1-85937-095-0	£9.99	Great Yarmouth (pb)	1-85937-426-3	£9.99
Cheshire (pb)	1-85937-271-6	£9.99	Greater Manchester (pb)	1-85937-266-x	£9.99
Chester	1-85937-090-x	£12.99	Guildford (pb)	1-85937-410-7	£9.99
Chesterfield	1-85937-378-x	£9.99	Hampshire (pb)	1-85937-279-1	£9.99
Chichester (pb)	1-85937-228-7	£9.99	Hampshire Churches (pb)	1-85937-207-4	£9.99
Colchester (pb)	1-85937-188-4	£8.99	Harrogate	1-85937-423-9	£9.99
Cornish Coast	1-85937-163-9	£14.99	Hastings & Bexhill (pb)	1-85937-131-0	£9.99
Cornwall (pb)	1-85937-229-5	£9.99	Heart of Lancashire (pb)	1-85937-197-3	£9.99
Cornwall Living Memories	1-85937-248-1	£14.99	Helston (pb)	1-85937-214-7	£9.99
Cotswolds (pb)	1-85937-230-9	£9.99	Hereford (pb)	1-85937-175-2	£9.99
Cotswolds Living Memories	1-85937-255-4	£14.99	Herefordshire	1-85937-174-4	£14.99
County Durham	1-85937-123-x	£14.99	Hertfordshire (pb)	1-85937-247-3	£9.99
Croydon Living Memories	1-85937-162-0	£9.99	Horsham (pb)	1-85937-432-8	£9.99
Cumbria	1-85937-101-9	£14.99	Humberside	1-85937-215-5	£14.99
Dartmoor	1-85937-145-0	£14.99	Hythe, Romney Marsh & Ashford	1-85937-256-2	£9.99

Available from your local bookshop or from the publisher

Frith Book Co Titles (continued)

Ipswich (pb)	1-85937-424-7	£9.99	St Ives (pb)	1-85937415-8	£9.99
Ireland (pb)	1-85937-181-7	£9.99	Scotland (pb)	1-85937-182-5	£9.99
Isle of Man (pb)	1-85937-268-6	£9.99	Scottish Castles (pb)	1-85937-323-2	£9.99
Isles of Scilly	1-85937-136-1	£14.99	Sevenoaks & Tunbridge	1-85937-057-8	£12.99
Isle of Wight (pb)	1-85937-429-8	£9.99	Sheffield, South Yorks (pb)	1-85937-267-8	£9.99
Isle of Wight Living Memories	1-85937-304-6	£14.99	Shrewsbury (pb)	1-85937-325-9	£9.99
Kent (pb)	1-85937-189-2	£9.99	Shropshire (pb)	1-85937-326-7	£9.99
Kent Living Memories	1-85937-125-6	£14.99	Somerset	1-85937-153-1	£14.99
Lake District (pb)	1-85937-275-9	£9.99	South Devon Coast	1-85937-107-8	£14.99
Lancaster, Morecambe & Heysham (pb)	1-85937-233-3	£9.99	South Devon Living Memories	1-85937-168-x	£14.99
Leeds (pb)	1-85937-202-3	£9.99	South Hams	1-85937-220-1	£14.99
Leicester	1-85937-073-x	£12.99	Southampton (pb)	1-85937-427-1	£9.99
Leicestershire (pb)	1-85937-185-x	£9.99	Southport (pb)	1-85937-425-5	£9.99
Lincolnshire (pb)	1-85937-433-6	£9.99	Staffordshire	1-85937-047-0	£12.99
Liverpool & Merseyside (pb)	1-85937-234-1	£9.99	Stratford upon Avon	1-85937-098-5	£12.99
London (pb)	1-85937-183-3	£9.99	Suffolk (pb)	1-85937-221-x	£9.99
Ludlow (pb)	1-85937-176-0	£9.99	Suffolk Coast	1-85937-259-7	£14.99
Luton (pb)	1-85937-235-x	£9.99	Surrey (pb)	1-85937-240-6	£9.99
Maidstone	1-85937-056-x	£14.99	Sussex (pb)	1-85937-184-1	£9.99
Manchester (pb)	1-85937-198-1	£9.99	Swansea (pb)	1-85937-167-1	£9.99
Middlesex	1-85937-158-2	£14.99	Tees Valley & Cleveland	1-85937-211-2	£14.99
New Forest	1-85937-128-0	£14.99	Thanet (pb)	1-85937-116-7	£9.99
Newark (pb)	1-85937-366-6	£9.99	Tiverton (pb)	1-85937-178-7	£9.99
Newport, Wales (pb)	1-85937-258-9	£9.99	Torbay	1-85937-063-2	£12.99
Newquay (pb)	1-85937-421-2	£9.99	Truro	1-85937-147-7	£12.99
Norfolk (pb)	1-85937-195-7	£9.99	Victorian and Edwardian Cornwall	1-85937-252-x	£14.99
Norfolk Living Memories	1-85937-217-1	£14.99	Victorian & Edwardian Devon	1-85937-253-8	£14.99
Northamptonshire	1-85937-150-7	£14.99	Victorian & Edwardian Kent	1-85937-149-3	£14.99
Northumberland Tyne & Wear (pb)	1-85937-281-3	£9.99	Vic & Ed Maritime Album	1-85937-144-2	£17.99
North Devon Coast	1-85937-146-9	£14.99	Victorian and Edwardian Sussex	1 85937-157-4	£14.99
North Devon Living Memories	1-85937-261-9	£14.99	Victorian & Edwardian Yorkshire	1-85937-154-x	£14.99
North London	1-85937-206-6	£14.99	Victorian Seaside	1-85937-159-0	£17.99
North Wales (pb)	1-85937-298-8	£9.99	Villages of Devon (pb)	1-85937-293-7	£9.99
North Yorkshire (pb)	1-85937-236-8	£9.99	Villages of Kent (pb)	1-85937-294-5	£9.99
Norwich (pb)	1-85937-194-9	£8.99	Villages of Sussex (pb)	1-85937-295-3	£9.99
Nottingham (pb)	1-85937-324-0	£9.99	Warwickshire (pb)	1-85937-203-1	£9.99
Nottinghamshire (pb)	1-85937-187-6	£9.99	Welsh Castles (pb)	1-85937-322-4	£9.99
Oxford (pb)	1-85937-411-5	£9.99	West Midlands (pb)	1-85937-289-9	£9.99
Oxfordshire (pb)	1-85937-430-1	£9.99	West Sussex	1-85937-148-5	£14.99
Peak District (pb)	1-85937-280-5	£9.99	West Yorkshire (pb)	1-85937-201-5	£9.99
Penzance	1-85937-069-1	£12.99	Weymouth (pb)	1-85937-209-0	£9.99
Peterborough (pb)	1-85937-219-8	£9.99	Wiltshire (pb)	1-85937-277-5	£9.99
Piers	1-85937-237-6	£17.99	Wiltshire Churches (pb)	1-85937-171-x	£9.99
Plymouth	1-85937-119-1	£12.99	Wiltshire Living Memories	1-85937-245-7	£14.99
Poole & Sandbanks (pb)	1-85937-251-1	£9.99	Winchester (pb)	1-85937-428-x	£9.99
Preston (pb)	1-85937-212-0	£9.99	Windmills & Watermills	1-85937-242-2	£17.99
Reading (pb)	1-85937-238-4	£9.99	Worcester (pb)	1-85937-165-5	£9.99
Romford (pb)	1-85937-319-4	£9.99	Worcestershire	1-85937-152-3	£14.99
Salisbury (pb)	1-85937-239-2	£9.99	York (pb)	1-85937-199-x	£9.99
Scarborough (pb)	1-85937-379-8	£9.99	Yorkshire (pb)	1-85937-186-8	£9.99
St Albans (pb)	1-85937-341-0	£9.99	Yorkshire Living Memories	1-85937-166-3	£14.99

See Frith books on the internet www.francisfrith.co.uk

FRITH PRODUCTS & SERVICES

Francis Frith would doubtless be pleased to know that the pioneering publishing venture he started in 1860 still continues today. A hundred and forty years later, The Francis Frith Collection continues in the same innovative tradition and is now one of the foremost publishers of vintage photographs in the world. Some of the current activities include:

Interior Decoration

Today Frith's photographs can be seen framed and as giant wall murals in thousands of pubs, restaurants, hotels, banks, retail stores and other public buildings throughout the country. In every case they enhance the unique local atmosphere of the places they depict and provide reminders of gentler days in an increasingly busy and frenetic world.

Product Promotions

Frith products are used by many major companies to promote the sales of their own products or to reinforce their own history and heritage. Frith promotions have been used by Hovis bread, Courage beers, Scots Porage Oats, Colman's mustard, Cadbury's foods, Mellow Birds coffee, Dunhill pipe tobacco, Guinness, and Bulmer's Cider.

Genealogy and Family History

As the interest in family history and roots grows world-wide, more and more people are turning to Frith's photographs of Great Britain for images of the towns, villages and streets where their ancestors lived; and, of course, photographs of the churches and chapels where their ancestors were christened, married and buried are an essential part of every genealogy tree and family album.

Frith Products

All Frith photographs are available Framed or just as Mounted Prints and Posters (size 23 x 16 inches). These may be ordered from the address below. From time to time other products - Address Books, Calendars, Table Mats, etc - are available.

The Internet

Already twenty thousand Frith photographs can be viewed and purchased on the internet through the Frith websites and a myriad of partner sites.

For more detailed information on Frith companies and products, look at these sites:

www.francisfrith.co.uk
www.francisfrith.com
(for North American visitors)

See the complete list of Frith Books at:

www.francisfrith.co.uk

This web site is regularly updated with the latest list of publications from the Frith Book Company. If you wish to buy books relating to another part of the country that your local bookshop does not stock, you may purchase on-line.

For further information, trade, or author enquiries please contact us at the address below:
The Francis Frith Collection, Frith's Barn, Teffont, Salisbury, Wiltshire, England SP3 5QP.
Tel: +44 (0)1722 716 376 Fax: +44 (0)1722 716 881 Email: sales@francisfrith.co.uk

See Frith books on the internet www.francisfrith.co.uk

TO RECEIVE YOUR FREE MOUNTED PRINT

Mounted Print
Overall size 14 x 11 inches

Cut out this Voucher and return it with your remittance for £1.95 to cover postage and handling, to UK addresses. For overseas addresses please include £4.00 post and handling. Choose any photograph included in this book. Your SEPIA print will be A4 in size, and mounted in a cream mount with burgundy rule line, overall size 14 x 11 inches.

Order additional Mounted Prints at HALF PRICE (only £7.49 each*)

If there are further pictures you would like to order, possibly as gifts for friends and family, purchase them at half price (no additional postage and handling required).

Have your Mounted Prints framed*

For an additional £14.95 per print you can have your chosen Mounted Print framed in an elegant polished wood and gilt moulding, overall size 16 x 13 inches (no additional postage and handling required).

---

* IMPORTANT!
These special prices are only available if ordered using the original voucher on this page (no copies permitted) and at the same time as your free Mounted Print, for delivery to the same address

---

Frith Collectors' Guild

From time to time we publish a magazine of news and stories about Frith photographs and further special offers of Frith products. If you would like 12 months FREE membership, please return this form.

Send completed forms to:
**The Francis Frith Collection,
Frith's Barn, Teffont, Salisbury,
Wiltshire SP3 5QP**

Voucher for FREE and Reduced Price Frith Prints

Picture no.	Page number	Qty	Mounted @ £7.49	Framed + £14.95	Total Cost
		1	**Free of charge***	£	£
			£7.49	£	£
			£7.49	£	£
			£7.49	£	£
			£7.49	£	£
			£7.49	£	£

Please allow 28 days for delivery	*** Post & handling**	**£1.95**
Book Title	**Total Order Cost**	**£**

Please do not photocopy this voucher. Only the original is valid, so please cut it out and return it to us.

I enclose a cheque / postal order for £ . . . .
made payable to 'The Francis Frith Collection'
OR please debit my Mastercard / Visa / Switch / Amex card
(credit cards please on all overseas orders)

Number . . . .

Issue No (Switch only) . . . . .Valid from (Amex/Switch) . . . .

Expires . . . . Signature . . . .

Name Mr/Mrs/Ms . . . .

Address . . . .

. . . .

. . . . Postcode . . . .

Daytime Tel No . . . .   Valid to 31/12/02

The Francis Frith Collectors' Guild

Please enrol me as a member for 12 months free of charge.

Name Mr/Mrs/Ms . . . .

Address . . . .

. . . .

. . . . Postcode . . . .

Would you like to find out more about Francis Frith?

We have recently recruited some entertaining speakers who are happy to visit local groups, clubs and societies to give an illustrated talk documenting Frith's travels and photographs. If you are a member of such a group and are interested in hosting a presentation, we would love to hear from you.

Our speakers bring with them a small selection of our local town and county books, together with sample prints. They are happy to take orders. A small proportion of the order value is donated to the group who have hosted the presentation. The talks are therefore an excellent way of fundraising for small groups and societies.

Can you help us with information about any of the Frith photographs in this book?

We are gradually compiling an historical record for each of the photographs in the Frith archive. It is always fascinating to find out the names of the people shown in the pictures, as well as insights into the shops, buildings and other features depicted.

If you recognize anyone in the photographs in this book, or if you have information not already included in the author's caption, do let us know. We would love to hear from you, and will try to publish it in future books or articles.

Our production team

Frith books are produced by a small dedicated team at offices in the converted Grade II listed 18th-century barn at Teffont near Salisbury, illustrated above. Most have worked with the Frith Collection for many years. All have in common one quality: they have a passion for the Frith Collection. The team is constantly expanding, but currently includes:

Jason Buck, John Buck, Douglas Burns, Heather Crisp, Isobel Hall, Rob Hames, Hazel Heaton, Peter Horne, James Kinnear, Tina Leary, Hannah Marsh, Eliza Sackett, Terence Sackett, Sandra Sanger, Shelley Tolcher, Susanna Walker, Clive Wathen and Jenny Wathen.